The Unfinished Assignment: Equal Education for Women

Patricia L. McGrath

Worldwatch Paper 7
July 1976

This paper is adapted from a forthcoming book on the changing role of women worldwide. It may be partially reproduced with acknowledgement to Worldwatch Institute.

The views and conclusions contained in this document are those of the author and do not necessarily represent those of Worldwatch Institute, its directors, officers, or staff.

Preface

Patricia McGrath's "The Unfinished Assignment: Equal Education for Women" is another in a series of studies published by Worldwatch Institute. These papers are part of an ongoing effort to identify and analyze emerging global trends and to bring them to public attention. Previous issues in the series are listed inside the back cover.

Worldwatch Paper 7 traces the development of new educational opportunities for women around the world. Whether their success is measured by entrance into professional schools in industrialized countries or high school enrollment in developing societies, women are taking advantage of education to improve their social and economic positions in unprecedented numbers. Recent gains in women's literacy, formal schooling, and participation in the teaching profession suggest that, while many formidable inequities remain to be overcome, the steady advances in women's education augur well for the emergence of a social order in which the ideas and energies of women are fully expressed.

This paper is part of a broader project examining the changing role of women worldwide and its impact on politics, employment, economic development, and social structures. This analysis of what may prove to be one of the most important social transformations of this century will appear in a forthcoming book, to be written jointly with Kathleen Newland, the author of Worldwatch Paper 3, "Women in Politics: A Global Review."

Lester R. Brown
President, Worldwatch Institute

Table of Contents

Overview and Implications 7

The Historical Background 11

Women's Literacy 14

The Primary School Experience 18

Women and Secondary Education 21

Acquiring Technical Skills 25

Women in the Universities 27

Women as Educators 33

Full Equality in Education:
  Obstacles and Solutions 37

Notes 44

Nearly three centuries have passed since a noble Venetian, Elena Piscopia, a student at the University of Padua, became the first woman in history to receive a doctoral degree. Against the backdrop of two million years of human evolution, 300 years may sound like a barely audible sigh, but it has sounded like an indeterminate sentence to women bottled up by the traditional female role. For most of that interval women's educational status has improved very slowly. During the last quarter century, however, subtle changes have occurred. Far from the corridors of international conference halls or the pages of the press, in places as disparate as village councils and the Ivy League, the decision has been made to enroll more girls in school.

7

In some areas the trend toward equal education is well-advanced; in others, it is just beginning. Many obstacles remain to be overcome. Yet on the basis of the gains that have already been made, it seems fair to predict that equal education for women will shape the future, perhaps profoundly, for men as well as women.

Fifty years ago there were only 43 Egyptian girls attending secondary school; by 1971 there were half a million.[1] Since 1950, the female share of university enrollments has doubled in Japan, tripled in Nigeria, quadrupled in Pakistan, and quintupled in Thailand.[2] Since 1960, female enrollment at U.S. law schools has jumped from 3 percent to 20 percent; at three schools, female law students now outnumber males. These figures represent only the tip of the iceberg; the changes at the lower rungs of the educational ladder are even more significant and broadly based.

More of the world's women can now read and write than ever before. For many women, literacy has become a door into the twentieth century, a means of achieving social mobility and participating in the affairs of both their own communities and the wider world. The enrollment of females in primary and secondary schools has nearly caught up with that of males on every continent except Africa and Asia. Though university enrollments still trail behind, the most rapid gains are now being made at this level. Since higher education is the training ground for persons who will assume leadership positions, women's gains at the university level should have even greater implications for their roles in society than did earlier gains at the primary and secondary school levels.

Changes in women's actions and expectations tend to show up first and most markedly among the college-educated. Highly-trained women, who demand equal advancement and opportunity in areas traditionally monopolized by men, are the most sorely conscious of the disadvantages that afflict their sex. Women college graduates are the first to question the "Noah's Ark" configuration of the world, in which all animals must be paired. They are the first to experiment with new lifestyles, and are the most likely to dedicate themselves to a professional career. They have the lowest average number of children, sometimes electing to remain unmarried and child-free. They display the most active interest in women's rights, and present the most poignant challenge to traditional male-female role stereotypes.

The *implications* of such a challenge fire the imagination. What can it mean for the composition of the labor force, our principal institutions, male-female relationships, individual lifestyles, and human welfare? Ability, aptitude, and interests are already gradually supplanting gender as criteria for school admissions and as occupational determinants. The world is facing up to the fact that, in the words of a well-known feminist, "there are very few jobs that require either a penis or a vagina." True, an individual's sex is stamped on every cell of the body. But of 48 chromosomes, only one is different. On this difference society has based a complete dichotomy of male and female, senselessly assuming that the possession of a womb implies an exclusive sex-linked ability to wash diapers, bake cakes, and bandage scraped knees, or to hoe yams, grind corn, and fetch water. Nothing in the natural order of things makes any individual man a better doctor, political leader, or truck driver than any individual woman. In fact, if driver safety were made a criteria for hiring truck drivers, women might dominate the occupation.

As Caroline Bird has pointed out, in a few short years surprising numbers of American institutions have amended practices that coerced women into family roles. New York State stopped inquiring into a woman's reasons for wanting an abortion, and California into her reasons for wanting a divorce.[3] Most colleges have abandoned responsibility for the private lives of women students. More women are now single or divorced, more wives are self-supporting, more children are born out of wedlock, more sex is extra-marital, and more men are beginning to treat women as people rather than as objects or possessions.[4] Though these developments on the American scene are not currently as visible in other lands, they may indicate the direction in which the vanguard is marching. They at least represent one field of new possibilities for individual and social development. The doors now opening will never be closed again.

The relative status of the sexes is not a zero-sum game governed by a "seesaw principle"—that women up must mean men down.[5] Instead, it is quite likely that, as one sex becomes better off, both will benefit. However, a big shift in the lives of women necessarily impinges upon men and children, who must make certain compensatory adjustments. Will more women doctors and executives inevitably mean more male nurses and secretaries? Will maternity leaves and day-care centers become as widely institutionalized as social security and health benefits? Might employers be forbidden to discharge a woman employee for pregnancy just as they are now forbidden to discharge a man for military service? Will housework, gardening, and cooking follow in the wake of canning, clothes-making, and the care of the sick, which have already passed from unpaid "customary work" to wage work? Will the new world of sexual equality be a world of fewer marriages and more divorces? Inevitably, educating women will have pervasive effects that influence everyone.

The marriages of career women are less stable than the marriages of women financially dependent on their husbands.[6] Moreover, career women may feel less need to marry in the first place, especially if they intend to remain childless, as a small but growing number do. Because the world of work is still defined in male terms (a full-time, inflexible schedule is the norm), a worker's position as a family member gets no support whatever, making it increasingly difficult for any female worker to function as a parent—a partial explanation for declining birth rates, rising divorce rates, and growing numbers of "latchkey" children coming home to empty houses. The likelihood is not that men and women will swap roles, but rather that the nurturant parental role may decline altogether.

An old maxim suggests that, even among those sympathetic to the idea, educating women has been conceived of as a means to other ends: "When you educate a man, you educate an individual, but when you educate a woman, you educate a family and a nation." Now it is more commonly recognized that women merit an educa-

9

tion in their own right, that they are an integral part of families and nations. The beneficial side effects to other members of society are nonetheless considerable.

In almost every country, educated women have fewer children, healthier and better-educated children, than do uneducated women. Educated women are more favorably disposed to family planning because they understand it, and because they often want to hold on to their jobs. In Turkey and Egypt, the fertility level decreases as women's educational achievement rises, with the average family size of university degree holders between one-half (Egypt) and one-third (Turkey) that of illiterate women.[7] Educated women also achieve higher labor force participation rates, higher productivity, and higher earnings, probably because the types of employment available to them confer sufficient financial return, job satisfaction, and status to motivate them to combine motherhood with a career. In Turkey, only 3 percent of illiterate women work in non-farm jobs, compared to 70 percent of university-trained women. The same situation exists in Egypt and many other developing countries. Though the relationship between education and employment is not linear, as these statistics may suggest, the correlation is well substantiated.

Such fertility and economic activity rates clearly have desirable implications for women's status in the family—for their ability to share in decision-making about children's schooling and about family finances, for instance. Education lets women into "the system"; once there, they will have to make a difference.

Some education and some measure of economic independence appear to be the foundations for a sense of having a certain control over nature, for planning ahead, for openness to new experience, and for toleration of diversity. Up until now, socially imposed ignorance has been at the root of women's longstanding inability to control the fundamental conditions of their lives.

Women's quest for equality is entering a new phase; increasing female enrollments have become both cause and reflection of events in other arenas. Young women aware of newly extended occupational horizons are determining to fulfill their ambitions in competitive rather than exclusively supportive career roles. Many now expect men to share responsibilities in the kitchen, the nursery, and the supermarket. There is no reason to believe that these sentiments

"Socially imposed ignorance
has been at the root of women's
longstanding inability to control
the fundamental conditions of
their lives."

will remain confined to Europe and North America: among the educated classes in many countries, the old female stereotype is being knocked on its ear.

This paper attempts to capture the flavor of these events in the educational arena. Education is a particularly appropriate place in which to seek evidence of changes in the way women think about themselves, because these changes are likely to register first in educational decisions: choice of schools, courses, and pre-professional qualifications. The trend toward higher female enrollments in graduate and professional schools may serve as a lead indicator of women's subsequent achievements in other areas such as employment and politics. Changes in female access to education both express other social transformations and provide an index of future alterations in fertility patterns, family status, marital behavior, and support for ideals of sexual equality. The recent increases in women's educational attainments are not merely a continuation of an existing trend; the change is already marked enough to qualify as a new trend in itself. Along with other groups of the erstwhile disenfranchised, women have pulled up a chair to the table, and show no signs of pulling back.

11

The Historical Background

Only a limited set of voices speak to us from the past: the literate and the elite. Missing is the testimony of the young, the impoverished, the uneducated, and the female. Life in the past was brutish and short, with little intellectual enlightenment for any but a small minority, regardless of sex. Even the great ages of learning—Classical Greece, the Renaissance, and the Enlightenment—for the most part passed women by. Plato was the first recorded feminist: in Book 5 of *The Republic* he advocated educating women like men. His idea met with derision at the time. Twenty centuries later, Plato's idea was still lying dormant as Rousseau wrote:

> The whole education of women ought to be relative to men, to please them, to educate them when young, to care for them when grown, to counsel them, and to make life sweet and agreeable to them.
>
> *Emile*

For most of recorded history, religion has been the driving force behind education. Often the first alphabets were developed by religious teachers, the first written manuscripts were religious texts, the first books were established by religious orders, and the main purpose of literacy was to facilitate religious teaching. Consistently, women's exclusion from religious duties and education robbed them of a public voice. As religion embodied the attitudes and social codes of the human beings who celebrated it—the male priests and scribes who gave it reality—the voice of God became the voice of man.[8] Even Christianity, with its early egalitarian ideals, quickly fell into the pattern of excluding women from full ecclesiastical equality. Saint Paul exhorted:

> Let your women keep silence in the churches; for it is not permitted unto them to speak; but they are commanded to be under obedience, as also saith the law.
>
> And if they will learn anything, let them ask their husbands at home; for it is a shame for women to speak in church.
>
> *Corinthians XIV, 34-5*

The modern investigator of female roles confronts a vast, uncharted ocean of silence stretching back into the past. Up until very recently, education in most countries, whether rich or poor, remained the prerogative of the elite, the wealthy—the fortunate few. It took place primarily in private homes or private schools, and for girls remained limited mostly to those arts necessary to attract a husband and to fulfill wifely duties.

Before industrialization, the individual's life was greatly influenced by membership in particular social enclaves: ethnic groups, tribes, extended families, and so forth. A person's class status, family affiliation, or sex could largely determine access to education, a spouse, wealth, and position; such factors were an overriding influence on each person's identity, activities, and aspirations. A beggar's child could not become a professor; an untouchable could not become a priest. Self-determination has been a monopoly of the upper classes.

Modern industrialization has given individuals the opportunity to become self-supporting outside their familial context, and has spurred the rise of "individualism" as a socially valued ethic. The extended family has slowly given way to the nuclear family. Individuals striving for success today have sought more years of education; they have married later, had fewer children, and moved frequently at the behest of employment opportunities. They have scurried after wealth, taste, prestige, and power in order to be able to answer the all-important social question, "Who are *you?*", shouted out at them by magazines, celebrities, and trend setters adept in the art of defining the desirable.

Ethnic, racial, and religious minorities, as well as exploited underdeveloped countries, have one by one rallied to the individualist and egalitarian standard of the modern age, claiming their turf as free and equal partners in society. Now women are following that lead, spurred on by a number of enabling factors.

Bit by bit, sexual equality promises to follow in the wake of other social movements like suffrage and civil rights, becoming "part of the Establishment, praised on principle, taught in the schools."[9] When eventually accepted, it becomes "unchallengeable, a plateau from which other actions can take off in time. Yesterday's radicalism becomes today's common sense."[10] Social conditions conspire to help people see the inequity of sex discrimination and the advantages of ending it. Medical technology has freed women from the biological imperative of constant and involuntary childbearing. Before birth control, men waited until they could support a family before marrying, and usually chose younger wives, a pattern reinforcing the patriarchal authority of husbands over wives. Now, postponing childbearing gives young wives a chance to look about themselves at a time when careers are being established, to consider a wider set of options than that which follows early motherhood.[11]

Medical advances have also prolonged the lives of women, so that most now have decades of potential working life beyond childbearing age, during which none of the limitations imposed on women make much sense.[12] Modern technology has taken work out of the home, and beckoned to women to follow it, for pay.[13] New technology has also eliminated much of the need for great physical strength in many occupations. Awareness is spreading as modern communications breach the barriers of tradition in even the most isolated communities. The sudden raising of global consciousness on women's issues by the media, as well as the proliferation of women's political organizations, lobbying efforts, writing, and legislative action are symptoms of the current ferment.

The answer to the all-important question "Who are *you?*" usually consists of an assertion of what an individual does for a living. Many women no longer wish to take a back seat in this matter, no longer wish to define themselves as an adjunct of someone else—a sister, daughter, wife, or mother of some man. They want careers of their own. Inevitably, the road to most prestigious careers winds through the hallowed halls or over the ivied walls of academia. Women have begun their climb. Predictably, they are now making the fastest gains at the university level, which is more directly career-related than secondary or primary school. In the latter, nearly equal admissions have been achieved on every continent except Africa and Asia, where economic modernization and full-blown individualism are still struggling to make themselves manifest.

The concept of mass education did not become widespread until just prior to World War II, and was not implemented until after the war. Concern for universal education was expressed in the U.N. Charter (1945) and in the Universal Declaration of Human Rights (1948), which state that men and women everywhere are entitled to basic rights and fundamental freedoms, including the right to education.

Progress toward universal compulsory education has proceeded unevenly around the globe, and has been marked by some sexual, economic, or ethnic discrimination virtually everywhere. Twenty years after the signing of the U.N. Charter, free and compulsory education was a legal requirement in only 89 of the 122 member states of the U.N. Educational, Scientific, and Cultural Organization (UNESCO). An estimated 43 percent of all school-age children do not attend school, and the majority of the unschooled are girls.[14]

Women's Literacy

Since 1950, world population has grown by about one and a half billion. That increment translates into more of everything human— more rich people, more poor people; more people well-fed, more hungry; more literate and more illiterate. Similarly, along the frontier of women's education, there has been simultaneous improvement and deterioration. A higher percentage of the world's women than ever before can now read and write. At the same time, the absolute number of illiterate women is greater than at any time in the past.

The decline in the percentage of illiterates is clearly encouraging for those who view literacy as a crucial factor in improving the general quality of human existence. But embedded in these figures is a trend that will dismay those specifically concerned with the status and future of women in society. For while the worldwide campaign to increase the number of literate adults is succeeding, the majority of the newly literate are male. Nearly two-thirds of the world's illiterate population is female. As the number of illiterate men rose by 8 million between 1960 and 1970, the number of illiterate women increased by 40 million, bringing the total number of women unable to read or write to half a billion.[15]

15

Many explanations have been offered for this retrograde trend. At the 1975 International Symposium for Literacy held in Iran, a UNESCO report pointed out that "illiteracy is caught in a vicious circle; not only is it a source of inequalities, but it is simultaneously the product of other inequalities in society—political, social, and economic." Ordinarily, education is regarded as a process that can serve humanity by fostering enlightened ideals, standards, and methods for dealing with human problems. Rarely is it realized that education is itself the product and reflection of a particular social setting, and that, as Paulo Freire has stated, "society shapes education in relation to the ends and interests of those who control the power." Those in authority, usually men, invariably direct educational resources toward their own interests: preservation of the status quo. By teaching social behavior as well as facts, schools channel boys and girls into traditional roles.

Freire's point goes far toward explaining the inequitable apportionment of educational resources between men and women. But the illiteracy of many women today is not simply a result of an autocratic policy imposed by those who control society. Access to literacy is governed by many factors besides sex. Age, religion, ethnic affiliation, economic class, and urban or rural residence all affect both men's and women's chances of becoming literate.

Within each geographical or ethnic grouping, however, female illiteracy invariably exceeds male illiteracy. The disparity is as much as

20 to 25 percentage points in Asia, Africa, and the Arab states, where female status remains relatively low; the discrepancy is anywhere from one to seven percentage points in North America, Europe, and Latin America. (See Figure 1.)

Figure 1: Male and Female Adult Illiteracy Rates, Around 1970

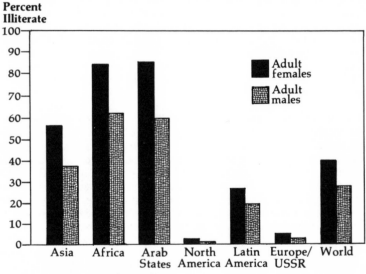

Source: Population Reference Bureau

The sexual differential is almost certainly worse than these figures suggest, because even the minimal ability to read and write one's own name is often accepted by census-takers as evidence of literacy. If the criteria were "functional literacy"—the ability to perform simple everyday tasks that involve reading and writing—an even higher percentage of women would be judged illiterate. The difference between female "literacy" and "functional literacy" is a product not of limited female access to formal educational facilities, but rather of women's relative lack of any "literacy environment," that is, opportunities and responsibilities in daily life geared to the uses of literacy. Thus many girls who do become literate eventually lose their skills for lack of practice.

Amid all these disappointing statistics, however, some encouraging trends stand out. Though the absolute number of illiterate women is increasing, the percentage of all women who cannot read or write is decreasing, from 45 percent in 1960 to 40 percent in 1970. In some countries, the literacy differences between older and younger female age groups have become striking. In Tunisia, for example, in 1966, 34 percent of women aged 15-19 were literate compared to 6 percent of women aged 24-34, and 3 percent of those aged 35-44.[16] In Algeria, Iran, Iraq, Kuwait, and Turkey, the differences in the literacy levels of the various age groups are also pronounced. Women clearly have farther to go than men in the elimination of illiteracy, but they are making progress.

In an effort to raise the educational level of their populations, many nations have begun to shift away from sole reliance on formal schooling (to which women's access has always been limited by conflicting role responsibilities) toward informal mass literacy drives, in which women often form the majority of participants. The International Institute for Adult Literacy Methods in Teheran now lists 790 organizations in 123 countries sponsoring grass-roots literacy efforts. In late 1974, the World Bank promised to commit one billion dollars over the following five years to spreading basic literacy skills. Many countries—including China, Cuba, Chile, Brazil, Somalia, Indonesia, and Bangladesh—have tried mass literacy campaigns, with mixed success. Reports from China confirm dramatic gains in female literacy since the revolution. Other countries have effectively used the mass media to combat illiteracy among rural residents and women, groups whose access to education has heretofore been limited.

Before the First World War, 88 percent of Russian women were illiterate and contemporary educators anticipated that it would take 250 years to universalize literacy in that country. In fact, in less than 50 years the task has been accomplished.[17] Leaders like the late Ho Chi Minh, intent on transforming their societies, often emphasize general literacy, and literacy for women in particular:

> Women should study all the more assiduously in order to make up for the countless obstacles that have prevented them from obtaining instruction till now. The hour has struck for them to catch up with men and to make themselves worthy to be full-fledged citizens.

> Quoted by le Thanh Khoi, 1975

17

In 1945, when Ho Chi Minh made the above declaration, 90 percent of the North Vietnamese population was illiterate. Today the rate of illiteracy is estimated to be about 6 percent.[18] This complete turn-about demonstrates the gains that can be made when literacy is made a high national priority.

18 Where men continue to be given preference in educational programs, women's minds are being bound as cruelly as once their feet were. The modern world is very much a world of words, and despite the new educational opportunities provided by radio and television, the illiterate person is severely handicapped.

The Primary School Experience

Because historical perspective sheds a diffused, mellowing light on many contemporary problems, the current status of females in primary education looks better if approached comparatively from the vantage point of thirty years past. In almost every country for which statistics are available, female access to primary education has improved greatly, with enrollments swelling from a mere trickle to near parity in many areas of the globe.

Today free and compulsory primary education for both sexes is a goal, if not already an actual policy, of almost every government. Even in the conservative Muslim society of Saudi Arabia, King Faisal opened schools for girls more than a decade ago, though a show of force was thought necessary to quell resistance to the idea. Females comprise nearly half of total primary school enrollments in five out of seven major geographical areas, and the world average is already well above 40 percent. (See Table 1.) As long ago as 1965, 58 of 122 members and associate member states of UNESCO had almost equal percentages of girls and boys enrolled in primary schools.

Untrammelled optimism on the basis of these figures is, however, premature. While girls' access to primary education improved greatly during the fifties, the pace has slowed since then. The female share of primary school enrollment worldwide rose only slightly between 1961 and 1970, from 42.5 to 43.6 percent. Though the female portion is about two-fifths in many countries, actual parity has been reached in only 14 of the 99 countries for which UNICEF has comparative statistics.[19] The share of girls of the appropriate age actually attending primary school varies widely, from as little as one third in Africa, to nearly nine out of ten in Europe and North America.

Table 1: Female Share of Primary School Enrollment, 1970

Region	Percent
North America	49.4
U.S.S.R.	49.0
Europe	48.7
Latin America	48.6
Oceania	47.6
Africa	39.7
Asia*	38.1
World	43.6

*Excluding People's Republic of China, N. Korea, N. Vietnam.

Source: Center for Integrative Studies, 1975. Based on U.N. Statistical Yearbook, 1973.

The gap in most developing countries between the theoretical inclusion of girls and women in education systems and their actual integration is often wide. While girls before the age of puberty might attend some or all of the primary school grades in a compulsory education system, their numbers decline more rapidly than those of boys as they approach secondary school. Often the highest rate of female desertion occurs over summer vacation—between school cycles, not during them—suggesting that girls must overcome different social obstacles than must boys, including parental disapproval.[20] More than half of the countries that furnish UNESCO with information consider the female drop-out problem to be one of the gravest difficulties confronting their national goals in primary education.

The higher drop-out rate for girls is particularly prevalent in those African and Asian societies in which gradual acceptance of primary education for girls has not been accompanied by any radical alteration in parental expectations for daughters. In these societies, some families are now more inclined to educate their daughters up through primary level only because it is considered prestigious to do so, or because educated men seem to prefer wives with some schooling. The potentially liberating effects of female education are diluted as girls who are encouraged to acquire basic skills in reading, writing, and arithmetic are simultaneously discouraged from putting their skills to any use that might be incompatible with early marriage or seclusion.

Even where female enrollments have increased manyfold, fewer than 10 percent of the primary-school-aged girls may actually be in school. In Afghanistan, Bangladesh, Bhutan, Ethiopia, Malawi, New Hebrides, and Upper Volta, among others, the enrollment increases are measured from abysmally small beginnings. The Yemen Arab Republic still has the world's lowest rate of female attendance: only one girl out of a hundred ever attends school.[21]

Attendance is not the only problem. Even where female primary school enrollment approaches 50 percent, girls' horizons are being limited by the imposition of role stereotypes. By the time American girls reach fourth grade, their visions of occupations open to them are largely narrowed to four: teacher, secretary, nurse, or mother. Boys of the same age do not view their occupational potential through such restrictive glasses.[22]

Instead of anticipating social change, and preparing children to live in the society of the future, primary schools reflect current or even outdated social patterns. Often, therefore, schools become mechanisms for social control, and perpetuate conformity, social stratification and dependence on others for learning. Young girls excel academically partially because elementary school values are congruent with the traditional demands of the female sex role. Primary education reinforces obedience, social and emotional dependence, and docility. Subsequently, girls become prisoners of their own experience and others' expectations.

For any child, primary school is an important entree to broader experiences and awareness of events in the public domain. In societies in which women's contacts remain otherwise circumscribed, literacy and primary schooling may be even more important for them than for men, since men are routinely expected to interact with other adults in the course of employment, recreation, political participation, and

"Girls become prisoners of
their own experience and others'
expectations."

religious observance. Where such informal learning situations for women are severely limited, compulsory education can be a key to the development of independent values and to future gains in status.

Primary education is a prerequisite for further educational attainment, which in turn strongly influences eligibility for independent roles in adult society. Increased female primary school enrollments since the Second World War represent a flying wedge into the barriers that block women's achievement and an opening to the rights and prerogatives that lie beyond. But much remains to be accomplished.

21

Women and Secondary Education

While access to elementary education for girls meets with relatively little resistance, the situation is entirely different for education at the next higher level. Elementary education takes place before the age of marriage and the assumption of adult responsibilities. Furthermore, its content is "neutral"—it does not prepare the pupils for a specified role in society. In contrast, secondary instruction generally prepares adolescents for adult roles, often in teaching or trades. It is seldom compulsory, and usually involves parental decisions and financial commitments.

Acceptance of female secondary education is nevertheless gaining ground. The worldwide postwar expansion of school systems and student populations has also extended to the secondary level, and, as the total number of secondary students has increased, so too has the proportion of female students in some areas. Of 121 UNESCO member states filing data in 1967, 60 had attained more than 46 percent female enrollment in secondary education—a big improvement over the situation existing in 1950, when only 31 countries had passed that threshold. During the same time span, the number of countries having less than 20 percent female secondary school enrollment dropped from 14 to six.[23] In most cases, the number of girls has increased more rapidly than that of boys. In fact, in a few countries today, proportionately more girls than boys stay in school until the higher grade levels. In Finland, Sweden, Canada, and the United States, women have traditionally attained higher levels of education than men, as measured by median years of school completion.[24] In the United States, where girls have stayed in school to qualify for teaching jobs while boys have dropped out earlier to enter higher-paying manual trades, more girls than boys have graduated from high school every year since the Civil War.[25]

Yet such encouraging statistics apply only to a small minority of countries, and, even in those, women's equal enrollment does not guarantee them an equal education. Even where girls are legally entitled to the same opportunities to attend secondary school, the programs available to them are not always identical to those offered boys. The danger of discrimination in the curricula is particularly strong in non-coeducational schools. Though coeducation is widely accepted at the primary and university levels, it is more controversial for adolescents. Even coeducational settings do not guarantee equal education: sexist textbooks, tracking, and lack of serious intellectual encouragement reinforce traditional feminine stereotypes and discourage academic achievement by girls.

By 1970, 75 percent of all American girls graduated from high school —the same proportion as boys, but a greater absolute number.[26] However, the girls' electives were heavily concentrated in the humanities and social sciences, while many more boys opted for mathematics and the sciences. A study based on nationwide achievement tests released in 1975 by the National Assessment of Educational Progress shows that girls from ages 9 to 17 slowly but steadily lose academic ground to boys of the same age. The data indicate that with increasing years of schooling, the distance widens between male and female achievement in traditionally male subjects like math and science.

Though this sex-differential phenomenon cannot be explained conclusively, it has been argued that girls often score lower and achieve less in later years because society expects them to. Ironically, lower expectations are learned by girls as much in the school environment itself as elsewhere. For instance, one study of American school texts found that 69 percent of the people in illustrations were males and that 75 percent of the reading stories were about boys.[27] Males are also more heavily and visibly represented in athletic activities and team sports.

The public education system—the very heart of the American equal opportunity ideal—seems to be unwittingly nurturing and perpetuating the violation of egalitarian principles.[28] This possibility is made all the more serious by the fact that more years of public education

—from pre-school to adult education—have increased the importance of the schools as socializing agents. The implications for sexual equality are grave if schooling proceeds along traditional lines of sex-role stereotyping, though countries such as Sweden and the United States have officially adopted programs designed to eliminate sexism in education.

The experience of girls in U.S. secondary schools generally reflects the experience of their counterparts in other industrialized countries, with some modifications. In seven other developed countries, there is a disparity between female rates of secondary school completion and subsequent rates of university enrollment—a good indicator of squelched academic appetites.[29]

In Eastern Europe, the fact that many boys enter career-oriented vocational training schools before finishing secondary school accounts for the predominance of girls among secondary school pupils. In Denmark, Finland, Ireland, and Sweden, girls or their families seem disinclined to regard an occupational career or profession as a permanent element of a woman's life. Choosing a general academic secondary school permits girls to postpone making any decisions about future work.

Nevertheless, some progress is undeniable. The female percentage of secondary school enrollments has edged above 40 percent in every major geographical region except Asia and Africa. (See Table 2.)

Table 2: Female Share of Total Enrollment in Secondary Schools, 1970

Region	Percent
U.S.S.R.	54.8
North America	48.8
Latin America	48.4
Europe	47.1
Oceania	44.0
Asia*	34.8
Africa	32.2
World	43.4

*Excluding People's Republic of China, N. Korea, N. Vietnam.
Source: Center for Integrative Studies, 1975. Based on U.N. Statistical Yearbook, 1973.

This fact represents a decline from primary school statistics. Girls drop out as a result of early marriage and various economic imperatives. However, female absenteeism is much lower in secondary school than at the primary level, possibly because parents and students more willingly accept the restrictions associated with studies voluntarily pursued.

In the developing countries, the gap between "modernized" men and "traditional" women is aggravated by situations in which more boys than girls attend secondary school. Boys are given greater access to technical and scientific training, while the girls are restricted largely to domestic courses. In many countries, girls are still being taught traditional beliefs and methods by illiterate mothers while increasing numbers of boys are given a semblance of modern education by the schools. Females comprise only about a third of all secondary school students in Egypt, Iran, and Jordan; less than a third in Turkey, Algeria, Iraq, Morocco, and Tunisia; a fourth in Syria; and only a fifth in Libya and Saudi Arabia.[30] The sex differential in African secondary enrollment is another case in point. In countries in which girls comprise about a third of the total enrollment, their share of secondary school enrollment falls to one or two out of ten.

In increasing numbers, however, governments are trying to eliminate discriminatory practices and to bring women into the schools. Though female secondary enrollments are still almost always smaller than male enrollments, they are often growing more quickly. This is strikingly true in Libya and Saudi Arabia, and, to a lesser extent, in Jordan, Iraq, and Egypt. In Venezuela, the proportion of the adult female population with some secondary schooling grew eightfold between 1950 and 1970.[31] In Bangladesh, despite strong countervailing currents of orthodoxy, poverty, and strife, the female percentage of secondary school enrollment increased from 9 to 16 percent between 1950 and 1970.[32]

Another index of dramatic change may be found in a comparison of three generations made in Egypt during the sixties. Those who interviewed five hundred girls in Alexandria's secondary schools discovered that only 20 percent of the students' mothers, and less than 10 percent of their grandmothers, had had any training beyond primary school.[33] One wonders whether these girls' achievements in family, occupational, and public spheres will differ commensurately when measured against those of their immediate female forebears.

Although the present status of women in secondary education is demonstrably inferior to that of men, it is making headway. The completion of secondary school is by most standards the criterion that defines an "educated person." For an increasing portion of the world's women, the achievement of that standard is more of a possibility than ever before.

Acquiring Technical Skills

Equal opportunity in the job market will not be realized without equal opportunity in vocational training. The discriminatory cycle is self-perpetuating. It allows the educator to say "why should we train women when the unions and technical professions won't admit them?" and the unions and employers to respond, "we'd love to admit women, but we can't find any qualified ones in our field."[34]

For most countries in which the number of professional positions is limited, technical or vocational education is the training most relevant to the available types of adult employment. Emphasis needs to be placed upon vocational training for women in order to arrest their large-scale displacement through structural and technical changes in the economy. Unfortunately, the limited training facilities developed for women often reflect the existing social biases against women's pursuit of male-dominated occupations. As a result, women workers are concentrated in a limited group of poorly-paid jobs. Training programs for women are often handicapped by the absence of planned outlets for students' skills: training is simply not coordinated with the job market.

Socialist countries have proceeded farthest in preparing girls for industrial work. In Hungary and the USSR, respectively, 17 percent and 33 percent of the girls enrolled in vocational courses are preparing for industry. This compares with less than 3 percent in France and less than 1 percent in Argentina and the United States.[35] In Norway, Sweden, and Poland, boys are encouraged to join girls in studying domestic science (cooking, sewing, and home economics). Reports indicate gradual feminine infiltration of traditionally male technical sectors in Poland, despite some persistence of a stereotyped division of labor. Yet adult women seeking vocational education in socialist countries are still constrained by their singlehanded responsibility for all domestic tasks and childcare. Unfortunately, day-care centers are seldom adequate to meet demand.

The greatest educational inequality between men and women may be among the working class, for whom technical schools are an important source of vocational training. In Switzerland, for example, technical schools were closed to girls as late as 1967. Until recently, women in France were excluded from many technical and vocational secondary schools. In spite of current attempts in France and elsewhere to encourage female enrollment in vocational courses, the number of women who apply remains relatively low. French women comprise only a quarter to a third of the students in the various technical training institutes.[36] Though French women in industry account for nearly a third of the employed female labor force, they have minimal qualifications and consequently are more likely to receive lower wages. The existing system of education directs women toward acquiring skills that are not in demand and that they therefore will not use. While men in French technical schools can choose from more than 390 skills and trades, women are limited to 171.[37] The myth of "masculine" and "feminine" technical training has been slow to expire. "It is considered feminine to dye hair, but not to manufacture hair dyes."[38]

In seeming disregard for the proliferation of highly diverse technical occupations, girls in developed, non-centrally-planned economies who pursue vocational training continue to sign up for courses in domestic science—as many as two-thirds in the U.S., and almost half in Argentina. In Japan, where female participation in the labor force is high, women comprise less than 2 percent of the enrollment in technical colleges, but 85 percent of the enrollment in junior colleges, where more than four-fifths of them major in home economics, education, or the humanities.[39] Japanese boys, on the other hand, select more marketable technical skills or attend the more prestigious four-year colleges.

In general, the same situation prevails in less developed countries in Asia, Africa, Latin America, and the Mediterranean. In Greece, India, Chile, and North Vietnam, typically only a fourth or a fifth of vocational enrollment is female. Even that number is predictably concentrated in domestic studies, which seldom lead to gainful employment and relate to only a small part of women's work and, consequently, of women's needs.

A cynic might describe women's technical training worldwide as training to be underpaid and obsolete, training for the "female ghetto" of

"A cynic might describe
women's technical training
worldwide as training to be
underpaid and obsolete."

sex-stereotyped jobs. But as working women become more aware of their disadvantaged condition and governments respond to demands for reform, some amelioration of this injustice can probably be expected. Almost everywhere the minute percentages of females receiving agricultural education stand in striking contrast to the high percentage of female agricultural laborers. Yet even conservative South Yemen has recently built a school to teach 3000 girls to drive and repair tractors, trucks, and fishing boats, as well as to master carpentry, masonry, building, and mechanical skills.[40] The University of the Philippines at Los Baños is now training nearly as many female as male agricultural extension agents. In the United States, the Percy Amendment to the Foreign Assistance Act, a legislative effort to orient foreign aid programs toward providing opportunities for women, also indicates growing governmental concern with women's exclusion from the kind of economic opportunities that technical training provides.

Women in the Universities

University education is but another stage in a woman's entire educational process, a process that begins with her earliest impressions of family organization and proceeds perilously through the tracking and "femininity training" that become most pronounced in secondary school. In most countries, higher education is the training ground for those who will take over the positions of political, scientific, and industrial leadership. Only to the extent that women can freely undertake advanced studies will they become qualified to assume responsibility in any of these fields. Despite the fact that male and female primary school enrollments are nearly equal in many countries, and that parity in secondary school enrollments has also been reached in some, there are few countries today in which the share of female students reaches 45 percent at the advanced level.

Yet no legal barriers stand in the way of women's higher education. Indeed, some military academies and ecclesiastical seminaries that until recently barred women are beginning to liberalize their admission policies, albeit under pressure. Though formal obstacles to equality in education are being swept away, informal and entrenched ideological constraints remain strong.

Low female enrollments in post-secondary courses are the result of social and economic obstacles; they also reflect the relatively small number of girls successfully completing primary and secondary schools. In several countries, female college students can be recruited only from a tiny qualified pool, often on the basis of difficult competition and sometimes in the face of insurmountable prejudice.[41] In others, such as the United States, the pool of potential female applicants is large, but equal female university enrollment and commensurate female achievement remain unlikely as long as the university is seen as a springboard into a world of business, administration, and professions that still excludes women.

28

Nevertheless, since the Second World War, women's educational opportunities in the university and professional spheres have expanded appreciably. Between 1955 and 1963, in 93 percent of the countries and territories studied by UNESCO, female enrollment increased, often dramatically.[42] By 1970, U.N. statistics show that women comprised the majority of university students—55 percent—in the Philippines, and above 45 percent in Poland, Finland, and the USSR. In the majority of European countries, the number of female university students doubled or tripled between 1960 and 1968.

In many African, Asian, and Latin American countries, the number of female university students has risen quickly from an initially low level. In Libya, the female ratio at the university level has risen from a meager 2 percent in 1960 to 11 percent in 1970.[43] In a number of African countries, female university enrollments have multiplied from seven to sixteen times. Though women still comprise only a quarter to a third of total university enrollment in most of the third world, their numbers are increasing.

However, women's share of university enrollment is between 40 and 50 percent in only two out of seven major geographical areas, and is consistently lower than female secondary school enrollment everywhere. (See Table 3.)

The percentages of college-age females enrolled in higher education remain surprisingly small, and again represent a dramatic decline from the percentages participating at the secondary level. In the United States, for example, between 75 and 90 percent of the "well-qualified" students who do not go on to college are women.[44] This represents a tremendous loss, in terms of both the social costs of misused human resources and the personal costs to individuals who sacrifice their eligibility for many rewarding and challenging positions.

Table 3: Female Share of Total Enrollment, by Level, 1970

Region	Primary	Secondary	University
. . . . percent			
North America	49.4	48.8	41.2
Asia*	38.1	34.8	27.7
Oceania	47.6	44.0	30.3
U.S.S.R.	49.0	54.8	49.0
Europe	48.7	47.1	35.5
Africa	39.7	32.2	25.9
Latin America	48.6	48.4	35.4
World	43.6	43.4	38.0

*Excluding People's Republic of China, N. Korea, N. Vietnam.
Source: Center for Integrative Studies, 1975. Based on U.N. Statistical Yearbook, 1973.

The availability of higher education to women in any given country does not always correspond closely with that country's level of economic development. The Philippines and Thailand, though less economically developed than most Western nations, have a higher percentage of female enrollment in their universities than do the nations of Europe. Educational opportunities for women seem to be largely a product of historical accident, governmental decisions, and national priorities. Economic development brings with it greater resources, and thus provides more flexibility in making public investments in a variety of social welfare enterprises. Whether revenues will be heavily invested in education and the extent to which women will benefit from this expansion are open questions.[45]

In the United States—a country with a high GNP—women's access to higher education has fluctuated rather than steadily improved. A peak was reached in 1930 and again in 1944, when American women received more than 50 percent of all bachelors and masters degrees. Then a sharp postwar decline set in as veterans swelled college enrollments. With the war's end, educators, journalists, and economists, fearing a glutted labor market, admonished women to leave their wartime jobs.[46] The press glamorized domesticity and full-time motherhood as they never had before. Individuals reacting against the deprivations of the thirties and the upheavals of the forties sought security in family life during the fifties; it became an atypical decade for women—a decade of retreat both from the labor force and from higher education.

30 Not until 1968 did American women again receive the proportion of B.A. degrees that they had earned in 1940. At that date their percentage of doctoral degrees still fell short of the share they had earned at the beginning of the Depression. The improvement in the female percentage of American Ph.D.s has been relatively steady but slow in recent decades, up from 10 percent in 1950 to only 19 percent in 1974. (See Figure 2.) None of the indicators of educational achievement examined by the U.S. Census Bureau—attainment, enrollment, field of study, or degrees awarded—shows that women have reached the same levels as men. But in most areas the educational gap between the sexes has narrowed since 1950.

A 1973 report by the Carnegie Commission on Higher Education, for instance, concludes that now and in the past American women have been disadvantaged as individuals in higher education.[47] According to the report, discrimination against women exists in admission to college, in acceptance into graduate school, in acceptance into and promotion within faculties, and in salaries paid. Alice Rossi, using data from a 1964 survey of forty thousand 1961 graduates, found that ambitious women who aspire to careers meet subtle and overt forms of discouragement rather than encouragement and support.[48]

In Britain, Oxford admits women, but they account for just 21 percent of the enrollment under a quota system and face different examinations from those given men. Prestigious awards, most notably the Rhodes scholarships, have been open only to men. When Cecil Rhodes, Britain's great empire builder and noted misogynist, died, he left behind a testament that embodied his imperial vision: bringing young men from America and the British colonies to Oxford.[49] Half the human race did not figure in Rhodes' dream of a world elite exposed to the best of British schooling.

A seemingly universal assumption that men and women have very different intellectual aptitudes manifests itself in a global intellectual

Figure 2: Percent of Bachelors, Masters, and Doctoral Degrees Conferred on American Women, 1900-1970

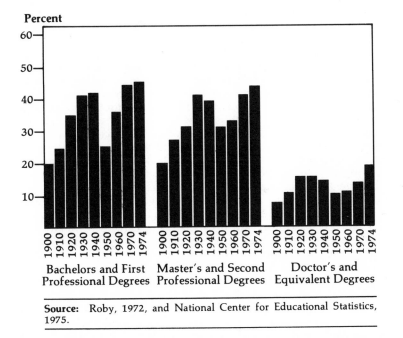

Percent

Bachelors and First Professional Degrees   Master's and Second Professional Degrees   Doctor's and Equivalent Degrees

Source: Roby, 1972, and National Center for Educational Statistics, 1975.

division of labor. Despite the increases in female enrollments and the spread of coeducation, sharp differences show up in the distribution of male and female students among the various academic disciplines. The subjects considered appropriate for women or men differ somewhat from one society to another. For example, medicine and dentistry are male preserves in the United States, while they are dominated by women in Poland and the USSR.

In general, women continue to be over-concentrated in the humanities and social services, while many of the more prestigious and remunerative disciplines, particularly the sciences, are reserved for men. The scarcity of female engineers and physicists may result at least partly from the notion that a woman's real career is likely to be marriage, and that her education is therefore more of a diversion than a serious preparation for earning a living. For many women, education remains a consumer good rather than a productive asset.

A few countries have attempted to overcome these cultural stereotypes by setting up programs to attract girls to exclusively male fields. Elsewhere, women have begun to seek admission to traditionally male departments as they become aware of the higher rewards associated with those specialties. In the United States, the enrollment of women in law schools has been increasing steadily for a decade and a half, and is now about a fifth of total enrollment—up from 3 percent in 1960, and 10 percent in 1970. The enrollment at Columbia University's business school is now 35 percent female, up from 5 percent in 1970. At Stanford University, the percentage of first year women interested in engineering has turned sharply upward in the seventies, rising from 1 percent in 1972 to nearly 6 percent in 1975. According to a survey of American medical school deans, about one-third of medical students will be women ten years from now, up from the present 18 percent. An exhaustive survey of freshmen at 366 U.S. colleges in the fall of 1974 concluded that 17 percent of women in their first year of college are now planning careers in business, engineering, law, or medicine; this figure nearly tripled in ten years.[50] In some cases, the dramatic increases simply reflect increased female applications; in others, admission policies have been reformed, and female "quotas" raised in response to increasing demands for equity.

As more women are accepted by universities and professional schools, more may realistically aspire to high achievement, and more young women will explicitly choose academic and professional careers over traditional female occupations. As the most highly visible and successful women in the media and in leadership positions focus attention on the positions women can aspire to, fewer and fewer girls will be willing to settle for less.

The upward trends are impressive, but a lot of ground must be covered before women will achieve parity in the professions. Fewer than five hundred of the American doctorates in computer science, fewer than six in a hundred in business management and architecture, and fewer than two in a hundred in engineering were awarded to women in 1974.[51] During the same year, no women at all earned doctorates in about fifteen fields ranging from Middle Eastern studies and Biblical languages to nuclear physics, metallurgy, and analytical chemistry.

"For many women, education
remains a consumer good
rather than a productive asset."

The negative employment implications of women's lack of specialized academic training are underscored by the high employment statistics for those women who do receive higher degrees. Ninety-one percent of the American women who received doctorates in 1957-58 were employed in 1964, and 79 percent of them had not interrupted their careers during that time, undercutting the oft-repeated prejudice that women are poor employment risks because marriage and childbearing undermine job stability.[52] Women's increasing enrollment in universities, and women's growing tendency to opt for competitive, pre-professional courses probably provide the best available measure for future equality in adult status.

33

Women as Educators

Despite the close association of education, especially higher education, with liberal progressive thinking, academia is in fact a stronghold of sex discrimination. Determination of the educational objectives of most societies remains in the hands of men. Women have had as little say in the educational decision-making process as they have had in making any of the major decisions affecting society as a whole.

In many countries, as a certain level of education has become universal and compulsory, teaching at the lower echelons has been entrusted to women. Primary education has become a female domain —firstly, because interaction with young children is consistent with traditional feminine roles and, secondly, because increasing numbers of teachers have been required to implement universal primary education programs.

Remuneration at the lower levels of the teaching profession, now occupied predominantly by women, is below that of the profession as a whole, as well as below that of most other professions requiring an equivalent amount of schooling. In the U.S., union membership among teachers is recorded at fewer than one in ten.[53] Low salaries have often been excused because it is expected that they will be supplemented by a husband's income. For this reason few men are attracted to these positions.

Beyond the primary grades and outside of the formal school system, women have held relatively few positions as educational agents. Almost universally, the proportion of women teachers declines with increasing rank. A review of selected large countries underlines the pervasiveness of this trend. (See Table 4.)

Table 4: Female Percentage of the Teaching Force, by Level, for Selected Countries, Around 1970

Country	Primary	Secondary	University
	. . . . percent		
India	25	30	15
U.S.S.R.	71	68	n.a.
U.S.	88	48	24
Japan	55	24	12
Brazil	90	54	21
Nigeria	23	19	10
Bangladesh	2	7	n.a.
Pakistan	24	27	23
West Germany	56	33	n.a.
Mexico	61	20	13
United Kingdom	77	44	n.a.
Italy	78	60	7
France	68	41	n.a.
Philippines	78	67	49
Thailand	34	24	40

Source: U.N. Statistical Yearbook, 1974, and others.

The few exceptions to this rule of male ascendancy are easily explained. In India, Bangladesh, and Pakistan, females comprise a higher proportion of secondary school teachers than of primary school teachers because in these societies cultural biases militate against the residence of female teachers in isolated rural grade schools. Secondary schools, however, tend to be more centrally located and to offer more acceptable accommodations. In addition, other factors, including overall job scarcity and the high prestige accorded to teachers, have kept primary school teaching attractive to men in these countries.

Even where women dominate the faculties at certain educational levels, they are less likely than men to reach administrative positions.

In the Soviet Union, women account for one quarter of the doctoral degrees, and nearly half of all scientific workers, but only one in ten of the senior professors or the members of the Academy of Sciences is a woman. Nearly 75 percent of Soviet school teachers are women, but only one quarter of the principals in the primary and secondary schools are women.[54] Such figures undercut Moscow's contention that it is far ahead of the West in granting women equality.

In Poland, the vast majority of secondary school teachers are female, but the proportion of men who become school principals is almost four times as high as the percentage of women who do so.[55] In France, more than half of the secondary school teachers were women in 1970, but the higher administrative positions within the *lycées* were dominated by men.[56]

Ironically, Islamic ideas about sex-segregation help to promote the employment of women teachers to some extent, since girls, if they are to be taught at all, must be taught by women. Many private schools in the Muslim countries are founded and managed by women. Currently, half of the Saudi Arabian primary school teachers are women, but only five women teach at the university level.[57]

In the United States, two academic employment trends merit noting: the proportion of faculty members who are women *decreases* with increasing rank and the difference in median salary by sex *increases* with increasing rank. The proportion of women in college and university teaching has declined—from a peak of 30 percent in 1944 to less than 25 percent in 1970.[58] However, to the extent that female gains made during the thirties and forties were tied to the Depression and to male absence during World War II, the more recent figures should not be compared unfavorably.

The women who do stake out their careers in higher education are generally excluded from what is predominantly a male communications and information system—the "Old Boy Network." Women comprise a meager 8 percent of full professorial appointments if religious and community colleges are included, but a mere 2 percent in the most prestigious universities. As Bernice Sandler of the Association of American Colleges wryly observes, the best way for a woman to become a college president is through the nunnery. The percentage of women teaching at the college level has not kept pace with the increasing rates of college attendance and graduation of American women.

In 1973, women constituted about one quarter of the staffs of U.S. institutions of higher education, being distributed principally at small colleges and universities and in the lower ranks of other institutions.[59] They tended to be concentrated in such fields as education, home economics, nursing, and social service.

Pre-eminent among the reasons for the poor representation of women in the higher echelons of the professional world is a cultural ambivalence toward any female attempts at combining career and family. Women who attempt to succeed in professional life must do so against the tide of popular opinion, while men with high career goals are propelled forward by the very swell that holds women back.

University hiring policies, reflecting the prevailing cultural mores, put endless hurdles and obstacles in the path of any female would-be academic. Male professors tend to hire men like themselves who have traveled the same favored career path. Because academic women cannot always study or pursue their research full-time, because they cannot always move to wherever the best jobs are currently available, and because anti-nepotism rules often prevent them from holding bona fide university jobs at all, they have a hard time competing against academic men under the present rules of the game.

A classic illustration of the insidious effects of anti-nepotism rules on academic women, Dr. Maria Goeppert Mayer, the only woman since Dr. Marie Curie to win the Nobel Prize in physics, once worked as a "volunteer associate" at Johns Hopkins University in order to continue studying physics. She could not be paid because her husband was on the faculty, but the University did not object to her working for free. Sensing the resentment toward women in American academic life, she learned to be inconspicuous.[60]

While the percentages of women teachers in primary and secondary education remain high, opportunities for advancement in these areas are heavily weighted in favor of men. Far more men than women are principals, superintendents, and school administrators. In 1975, HEW officials reported that women comprised two-thirds of U.S. elementary and secondary school teachers but less than a seventh of the administrators.[61] Three percent of junior high school principals, 1 percent of senior high school principals, and 0.1 percent of local school superintendents were women.[62] These figures reflect a negative trend: in 1928, 55 percent of elementary school principals were women, whereas in 1973, only 22 percent were women.[63] A random sample of 400 vocational school directors revealed that men hold 93 percent of all these top administrative positions.[64]

Equal opportunity and affirmative action legislation has begun to turn things around in some countries. With universities dependent on government contracts, and governments determined to enforce anti-discrimination laws, university administrators will be forced to alter their policies toward women. Respected journals like *Science* have analyzed the extent of sex discrimination in academia, and respected leaders have spoken out against it. There is growing evidence that the movement toward equality will persist until it has brought forth substantial changes in the academic establishment and in other professions. The demands for equality will persist not only because substantial injustices have been wrought, but also because women's career expectations are changing. Educational options for women are both a cause and a reflection of women's accession to a place in the wider world.

Full Equality in Education: Obstacles and Solutions

Most obstacles to full equality in education exist only in peoples' minds, in the insubstantial, diaphanous forms of prejudice, traditional beliefs, and cultural stereotypes. This is at once reassuring and discouraging—reassuring in the sense that there is nothing immutable about intangible ideas, discouraging in the sense that traditions tend to change much more slowly than do laws, government policies, or fiscal priorities.

Equal education for women is hampered by a whole set of mutually-dependent ideas and traditions that define and limit the female role. In developing countries, the acute shortage of educational facilities, in combination with a belief that boys should be educated first, effectively excludes many girls. Where there are few schools, students ordinarily must be prepared to travel some distance or to board, and girls' attendance is limited by beliefs that they should not travel alone or live apart from family supervision. In poor families, children's labor often contributes vitally to the economic viability of the household. Girls' education is precluded or curtailed by the belief that it is more appropriate for daughters than sons to be responsible for time-consuming household chores, care of younger children, and, in some regions, farming or marketing activities.

In cultures that deem it necessary for husbands to be more educated than wives, girls' education is cut short by parents who fear limiting their daughters' chances for marriage. Where family honor is tied to norms of female seclusion and chastity, most families insist that their daughters refrain from any contact with males, even in a school environment. The high premium placed on female virginity encourages early marriage, another effective bar to women's higher educational achievement.

It is the norm in many social systems for a woman to be transferred at marriage from the authority of her father to the authority of her husband; thus, parents reason that any investment in a daughter's education will be lost to them. This reasoning sometimes prevails even in egalitarian China's rural communes. There, girls are not selected for higher training because the leaders of their work teams fear that they will marry outside the team and move away, taking their educational capital with them.

Where girls are considered to be an economic burden, because female tasks are unpaid and undervalued, a substantial dowry is often awarded to the groom at marriage to compensate for the economic liability he has assumed; in these societies, parents often sacrifice their daughters' education to avoid double expenditure. Patriarchal attitudes in many societies hold education for girls not only irrelevant to the traditional female roles of wife and mother, but also potentially disruptive. Education might alienate women from their environment and make them less submissive to the dictates of their male relatives.

Almost universally, lack of appropriate employment opportunities for educated individuals dampens enthusiasm for costly education. Where jobs are scarce, they tend to go to men first, so parents reasonably conclude that investment in education for their daughters is less certain of return than is education for their sons.

Because they must overcome additional social and cultural obstacles without comparable levels of family encouragement, social approval, or financial reward, fewer girls enter school. Those who do attend school tend to drop out sooner than their male counterparts. The existing disparities between male and female education are thereby reinforced; uneducated mothers have low educational expectations for their daughters, and a lack of trained women to act as agents of educational change fortifies the male domination of the educational *status quo*.

Government policies reflect the social milieu in which they are formulated. Although extensive investments in primary and middle school education in Ghana opened up places for females, the government did not increase women's opportunities at the secondary and university levels proportionately.[65] Under the British Government's system of student grants, married women students receive less support than married men. Lack of child care facilities in Britain and elsewhere make it difficult for women to reconcile the roles of student and mother.

In the industrialized countries, the obstacles to full equality in education are also ideological and culturally entrenched, but the availability of financial and organizational resources to combat them seems greater than in poorer countries. In many, although not all, industrialized countries the expansion in educational systems has brought about near parity of enrollments for girls and boys through the secondary school level and greater access for women to higher education. Yet the opening up of more places for women does not assure an equivalence in the educational experiences offered to girls and boys.

Clearly, most education takes place within a system that was developed for men and that has only partially adapted to accommodate the entry of women. More often than not, the educational system tends to reinforce and rigidify the given stereotypes and differential treatment of the sexes. Curricula, textbooks, classification of subjects on the basis of sex, and an unwritten code of conduct all work against women. In school books, girl figures are less numerous, less independent, or less prominent. The female roles portrayed—housewife, teacher, nurse, secretary—only reinforce cultural stereotypes. Such books do nothing to create a sense of community between men and women and nothing to teach boys and girls that they are fellow human beings capable of holding varied roles, many of them shared and interchangeable.

Sex-differentiated courses—literature, languages, sewing, and cooking for girls, but metal working, science, and mathematics for boys—place girls and boys on an uneven footing for giving equal consideration to the full range of vocational and career possibilities open to them. A de-emphasis of girls' athletic activities deprives many girls of an important means of learning certain cooperative and competitive habits, attitudes, and skills that would be helpful in their personal development and in their relationships with others.

40 Prejudice, cultural imperatives (particularly the roles presented to girls in early life), and the greater absence of relevant role models for women at the higher stages of academic life discourage women from making full use of their intellectual talents. As a consequence, the percentage of women declines at successive rungs on the academic ladder. Educational expectations for men and women remain unequal largely because marriage is still regarded as the ideal career for women, while the necessity of earning a living is drummed into males from an early age. In the United States, India, Japan, and Germany, among others, daughters are often sent to school primarily to cultivate their desirability as wives and not to prepare themselves for careers. Therefore, not surprisingly, girls continue to elect different study programs than do boys, leading to degrees with less vocational relevance.

An obligation confronting any advocate of equal educational opportunity is ensuring that channels exist for putting educational investments to work. Because of societal ambivalence toward anything that conflicts with the traditional wife-mother role, approval of female careers has lagged behind acceptance of female education. In the U.S. this lag persists despite the fact that two-thirds of working women are not living that kind of life: they are single, divorced, deserted, widowed, or married to men earning less than $7,000 a year.[66] Yet because their incomes are considered merely "supplementary," their work is underpaid and their advancement opportunities are limited. For many of these women, prevailing social values are irrelevant, if not completely inimical, to daily economic reality. Anti-discrimination laws, affirmative action programs, and the simple recognition that a society needs to utilize fully all available human resources should all help bring female employment opportunities in line with educational achievement.

Some of the solutions to the problem of inequality in education are obvious; none of them is necessarily easy. Equal access to existing educational facilities and positions would be a first step. Equal access to non-academic employment, which would justify the time and financial investment in education, is also crucial. Equal pay for equal work would give women more incentive to work and would reinforce the logic of their doing so.

The double burden of working women needs to be recognized. Too often time-consuming household tasks are the last to be recognized as social obligations to be shared and are the last to be addressed by government programs. A comprehensive range of child-care facilities would help give adult women the free time needed for studies. In developing countries, widespread use of simple technical devices like water pumps, hand-operated grain mills, and wheelbarrows would greatly expedite some of the most time-consuming traditional female chores.

41

Over time, governments can open more places in schools for girls, lessen the financial burdens associated with women's education, reform curricula and counseling to encourage girls to formulate nontraditional career goals, and ensure greater equivalence of educational experiences for girls and boys. Legislative reform, attendance scholarships, tax incentives, free books and uniforms, and residences for women teachers might all further educational equality. Teacher-training programs might be designed specifically to create female role models who can act as agents of change. In the industrial countries, sweeping corrective measures have begun to be enforced, but even legal steps require supplementation. Courses that teach both boys and girls basic cooking, housekeeping, repairs, and self-defense might be a good way to liberate students from unrealistic views of their sex roles in later life. Women should be appointed to senior faculty and administrative posts. The widespread institutionalization of part-time appointments and flexible scheduling would facilitate female access. Pregnancy and maternity leaves would provide some of the necessary recognition of women's dual roles. Ideally, the same sorts of flexibility would recognize men's family roles also. The rules on tenure and anti-nepotism might be altered to eliminate their discriminatory impact on women.

Learning comes more easily when the content and structure of courses are related to the needs and experience of the student. Though women's education should not be confined to traditional female tasks, an appropriate first step for teachers of poor and illiterate women might be to focus on real-life problems such as nutrition, child-care, family planning, marketing, and agricultural techniques. Informal functional literacy programs with flexible hours are the key to reaching rural working women. From the most basic to the most sophisticated level, curricula should be periodically reviewed to make sure that women's experience is given adequate treatment.

The removal of tangible barriers to women's education will accomplish little without a transformation of sexist attitudes toward and expectations for girls. The educational system is perhaps the only institution that can counteract the tenacious foundations of sexual inequality that are built into the minds of children through traditions handed down from generations past. Only a deliberate, planned, and sustained effort can begin to replace the inequitable, traditional value system with something more just and humane. From the earliest days, girls must receive as much encouragement as do boys. Their studies must be esteemed as highly and financed as generously, their intelligence, curiosity, and initiative as carefully cultivated. Anti-discrimination laws are a first step, but beyond that many hearts and minds will have to change for full equality to move from law to life.

The educational prospect for women *is* rapidly changing—this chronicling of inertia and foot-dragging notwithstanding. Evidence of pervasive and persistent inequality does not mean that gaps are not being narrowed. Encouraging reports from places as disparate as Poland, Egypt, Ghana, and Bangladesh herald the eventual crumbling of the educational double standard. But how fast is fast enough? According to U.N. statistical projections for education, the situation of girls is improving in many countries, and is often improving more rapidly than that of boys. But by 1985, substantial disparities will remain.[67]

The reasons for wishing otherwise are not just humanitarian ones. Most people are now aware of the enormous social, psychic, and economic costs of racial discrimination. The cost of keeping women down is also high; a society that neglects the education of its women deprives not only them but itself. Germaine Greer concludes:

> Ultimately, if women were to realize their true potential as independent persons and insist on contributing their . . . talents towards running the world—politics, business, technology as well as family life—civilization might be led towards maturity instead of annihilation . . . .

> *The Female Eunuch*

If women were to have the same kind and level of education as men, they would thereby acquire comparable ability to make critical and independent analyses of the world they inhabit. They would be able to make greater economic contributions and have a greater voice in allocating economic assets. They would be able to assume a more equal footing with male relatives in making decisions about family welfare and family roles. Women would be able to compete on a more equal basis for employment and leadership roles in society. A greater measure of economic independence would enable women to give their own needs and their children's needs suitable priority, and would allow them to assert their wishes, including wishes to limit the number of children in the family, more fully.

43

The reproductive patterns and employment patterns of educated women differ dramatically from those of uneducated women, with the educated almost always more apt to have smaller families and more apt to participate in the labor force—two tendencies almost universally recognized as positive contributions to human welfare. Educated women also raise educated children. Studies have shown such children to be more supportive of sexual equality than the children of uneducated mothers.

Any change in women's situation in society has wide ramifications, rippling through women's many spheres of influence. Efforts to change women's role, even to enlarge it, inevitably touch upon a sensitive domain of cherished values. But the case for equality is being well-argued, and, if justice is served, its proponents will be heard.

Notes

1. William Goode, *World Revolution and Family Patterns* (New York: Free Press, 1965) and 1974 U.N. Statistical Yearbook.

2. U.N. Statistical Yearbooks, 1954 and 1974.

3. Caroline Bird, *Born Female: The High Cost of Keeping Women Down* (New York: Simon & Schuster, 1971).

44

4. *Ibid.*

5. *Ibid.*

6. *Ibid.*

7. Nadia Youssef, "Women in the Muslim World," in Lynne B. Iglitzin and Ruth Ross, editors, *Women in the World: A Comparative Study* (Santa Barbara: Clio Press, 1976).

8. Eva Figes, *Patriarchal Attitudes: The Case for Women in Revolt* (Greenwich: Fawcett, 1970).

9. Gary Wills, "Feminists and Other Useful Fanatics," *Harpers*, June, 1976.

10. *Ibid.*

11. Caroline Bird, *op. cit.*

12. *Ibid.*

13. *Ibid.*

14. Evelyne Sullerot, *Women, Society and Change* (New York: McGraw-Hill, 1971).

15. Population Reference Bureau, "Literacy and World Population," *Population Bulletin*, Vol. 30, No. 2, 1975.

16. Nadia Youssef, *op. cit.*

17. Evelyne Sullerot, *op. cit.*

18. Swedish International Development Authority, "Women in Developing Countries—Case Studies of Six Countries," Research Division, Stockholm, 1974.

19. U.S. Committee for UNICEF, "Facts About Females and Education," IWY Fact Sheet, 1975.

20. Mary Elmendorf, "The Many Worlds of Women: Mexico," in Janet Giele and Audrey Smock, *Women in Society* (New York: Wiley, forthcoming).

21. U.S. Committee for UNICEF, *op. cit.*

22. National Education Association, "Education for Survival," Washington, D.C., 1973.

23. Nicole Frederich, "Access to Education at All Levels," *Annals of the American Academy of Political and Social Sciences*, January, 1968.

24. Martha Darling, *The Role of Women in the Economy* (Paris: OECD, 1975).

25. Caroline Bird, *op. cit.*

26. Janet Giele, "American Women in Transition," in Giele and Smock, *op. cit.*

27. *U.S. News and World Report*, October 20, 1975.

28. Janet Giele, *op. cit.*

29. Martha Darling, *op. cit.*

30. Nadia Youssef, *op. cit.*

31. Sylvana Maccan and Michael Bamberger, "The Effects of Employment and Education on the Status of Women in Venezuela," International Sociological Association, 1974.

32. Audrey Smock, "The Roles and Status of Women in Bangladesh," in Giele and Smock, *op. cit.*

33. William Goode, *op. cit.*

34. "Wanted: Anyone Hurt by Sex Bias in Vocational Training," *Civil Liberties*, June, 1976.

35. Janet Giele and Audrey Smock, *op. cit.*

36. Catherine Silver, "Sociological Analysis of the Position of Women in French Society," in Giele and Smock, *op. cit.*

37. *Ibid.*

38. Evelyne Sullerot, *op. cit.*

39. Japanese Ministry of Education, "Women and Education in Japan," Social Education Bureau, 1975.

40. Minority Rights Group, *Arab Women* (London, 1975).

41. Nicole Friderich, *op. cit.*

42. *Ibid.*

43. Nadia Youssef, *op. cit.*

44. Patricia Graham, "Women in Academe," *Science*, Vol. 169, 1970.

45. Audrey Smock, "Determinants of Women's Roles and Status," in Giele and Smock, *op. cit.*

46. Pamela Roby, "Women and American Higher Education," *Annals of the American Academy of Political and Social Science*, Vol. 404, 1972.

47. Carnegie Commission on Higher Education, *Opportunities for Women in Higher Education* (New York: McGraw-Hill, 1973).

48. Ruth Hawkins, "The Odds Against Women," in *Women on Campus: The Unfinished Liberation* (New Rochelle: *Change* Magazine, 1975).

49. Angela Stent, "The Rhodes: Still Blocked," in *Women on Campus: The Unfinished Liberation, op. cit.*

50. American Council of Education, UCLA.

51. National Center for Educational Statistics, "Post Secondary Education. Earned Degrees Conferred, 1972-73 and 1973-74. Summary Data," U.S. Department of Health, Education, and Welfare.

52. Helen Astin, *The Woman Doctorate in America* (New York: Russell Sage, 1969.)

53. Germaine Greer, *The Female Eunuch* (New York: McGraw-Hill, 1971).

54. Hedrik Smith, *The Russians* (New York: Quadrangle, 1976).

55. Magdalena Sokolowska, "Changing Roles and Status of Women in Poland," in Giele and Smock, *op. cit.*

56. Catherine Silver, *op. cit.*

57. Minority Rights Group, *op. cit.*

58. Beatrice Dinerman, "Sex Discrimination in Academia," *Journal of Higher Education*, Vol. XLII, No. 4, 1971, and National Center for Educational Statistics, *op. cit.*

59. Carnegie Commission, *op. cit.*

60. Caroline Bird, *op. cit.*

61. Jonathan Spivak, *Wall Street Journal*, June 4, 1975.

62. *Education Review*, 1974.

63. Recruitment, Leadership and Training Institute, "Women in Administrative Positions in Public Education," July, 1974.

64. Women's Equity Action League, Washington Report, December, 1975.

65. Audrey Smock, *op. cit.*

66. National Education Association, *op. cit.*

67. Ford Foundation, "That 51 Per Cent: Ford Foundation Activities Related to Opportunities for Women," Ford Foundation, 1974.

PATRICIA L. McGRATH is a Researcher with Worldwatch Institute. Until recently her work has focused on population issues and on economic and political discontinuities. She is currently writing a book about the changing role of women. Prior to joining Worldwatch, she conducted anthropological studies of women's roles in Latin America, in Africa, and as a Marshall Scholar at Cambridge University.